beaches (1)

you frown in your beautiful portrait,
appearing dead even at the time,
in a weak blue oval of enamel sky.
what's wrong, my little peach?
tonight a wolf's eyes will glow
violet in a forest you'll never see
in a place you can't know. is that it?
and, somewhere, is a whole beach
made of glass pebbles you will never
lie down on, nor will your skin reflect
its blue, green, white, and burn.

beaches (2)

the house is large and dark
with narrow rooms
i woke today unable to move my arms
and called for him

the house is a honeycomb
the truth is i feel robbed
of a sweetness laboured hard for

the house behaves
like a person hiding in a cupboard
with held breath
i hate for the inanimate
to get the better of me

today i walked the length of the beach
to the caves
and thought of him for some time
pathetic girl
how colourless a beach in the rain

my imagination my rage
quiet and unlike any other
said to him
you know a cave had another form
before the water came

beaches (3)

a sand timer holds enough sand
to last the duration of one human life
the oldest sand was already ancient
when the first amphibian crawled onto the beach
the term egg timer came to prominence
only with the need for cooked egg perfection
sand of three transformative minutes
a princess is trapped inside the sand timer
swallowing the contents
a beach filling her mouth
the princess likes her eggs scrambled
with chives and black pepper
she swallows the sand and thinks about that

traditionally hourglass sand wasn't sand
an hourglass is also a body
an hourglass body is specifically designed
for you to want to put your hands
around the smallest middle part
traditionally the material was
powdered marble and burnt eggshell
the princess fits in the sand timer so nicely
like a chick inside an egg
so much swallowing done
her stomach has become a beach
the yellow sphere in her centre
pouring through her smallest middle part

beaches (4)

the sky fell
in the manner of an avalanche
with all its occupants
my heart fell through my shoes
& dropped into the river
much to my surprise
my heart caused a wave
(navy blue basically black)
tall & elegant & curled
which my heart then surfed
the wave broke, the water swelled
covering everything in sight
covering my face
taking my voice with it
when evening came
following a very short day
my heart washed up
in the shallow waters
of the grey beach
much changed
among the detritus of aeroplane & satellite parts
it had an igneous look to it
smouldering at the centre
& smaller than before
a man
covering his dick with one hand
handed me my heart with the other
i refused it with a head shake
it smelled unfamiliar, sulphurous

it had been to places i hadn't
he looked down at it like an injured bird
humiliated
i began to cry
i found a large section of mirror
settled down in front of it
to have a companion in my sadness
only then did I see my chest
open & dark as if a tooth had been pulled from it
i walked to the water
to wash
to relocate my voice
the water sealed up the hole
in my chest
the man waded in
he wore my heart around his neck
on a strip of leather
the heat at its centre was gone
but i knew it as mine
from its shape & hardness
& the way my gummy chest
called out to it
with a low humming noise
my chest a moonlit fridge
in a sleeping apartment
and a clock ticking
my heart suited him
the way it banged his chest
as he walked

his second heartbeat
he collected floating objects
took the time to consider me
as one of them
then moved on into deeper water
the muscles of his shoulders
seeming to hide furled wings
or compressed parachutes
a sudden feeling swept over me
who needed a heart
better to have the space for one
the power of that
i saw a dog
in the shallow water
its nose hovering above the surface
it came to me
making desperate noises
i said
sweetheart
this is a confusing place
the fur along its spine settled down
we sat together
who knows how long
eventually we felt like empty bags
like gone-off meat
things absolutely forgotten
down the back of the world
we thought of yellow beaches
of sleeping then moving

from the sleeping spot
& leaving a residual warmth
we thought of our new ghostliness
our liquid selves
without resources or luck
when the sky would reappear
how we would redraw our edges then
and with what

beaches (5)

people
orbit the griever
like a star
that might explode

elsewhere
the scuba instructor
once again
dreams of
last christmas morning

when he found a woman
face down
in the sea
felt it
bubble in her lungs
when he breathed
into her mouth

in his dream
the sky
is always domed
like a lid
and yellow

beaches (6)

this morning i saw a bee
out so late in the year
and all alone

a few paces on
brand new
early december roses

beaches (7)

having never lived by the sea
i have never intuited
anything carried
on its breeze: sirens, mist,
laughter
as the crabs boil

beaches (8)

there are things
you can say absolutely
a man should not be able to bear the weight
of a refuse truck on his chest

a clear wobble of heat lingers at the front grille
snow falls in the suburbs

there are matters of less certainty
will the crab come back out of the same hole
when the sea retreats
what similarity between crabs and lightning

when waiting for help to arrive
is it better to reverse a refuse truck
off the chest of a man
or no

a sand crab should not be able
to burrow its eggshell body
backwards through wet compacted sand

is it a man or a body
has there been a switch
is he pushing through
a very narrow corridor
in what direction

a sand crab fishes for food
with a feathery antenna
this is the manifestation of hope

the air is full of white speckles
the man's white trainers
are facing in unnatural directions
the truck is a dragon
the scooter's spinning wheel is romantic in a way

go home
eat half of a large meal
feel as if albumen surrounds you
try to wash it off
settle down to an artichoke of a dream
peel back its browning scales
the middle
i wonder
is it very soft

beaches (9)

my commitment to the city
is being tried in absentia
to the countryside
(with my favourite castle)
there can be no doubt
my commitment to him
hides in the sewer
with the rats big as babies

i observe myself in a new dress
marvel at its hugeness
incline my head like a virgin
organs a perfect nativity scene
all placed and vital and very still
feet not in frame

at the theatre
i smell myself on my fingers
the girls are really going for it
in their silver masks
a thousand eyes eat me
here's what i feel
that i, a mere stranger
to their new movements
i, a perfect stranger to
the curve of their wet backs
am a dirty grain of sand

in the evenings i am an orb
at the windows of my rooms
my ladies whisper in corridors
the lavender is uniformly wild
as it bows to the storm
the fountain flies sideways

you know how it goes
i love to fuck
neither hand has six fingers
i'll admit this much
in the correct light
and at a specific time
my head becomes the head
of a yet to be identified
woodland creature
most likely a muntjac
their eyes are green at night
and they bark like dogs

beaches (10)

this interminable christmas
          most often i am alone at night
          in my blue room
which is my preference
most recent rumour is a ghost came in the night   to fellate him
because even the dead like to please and leave a token of their visit
          in this case
a black hair wrapped ten times around his penis
when the frost lifts a dirty smell comes off the river and in through the windows
ghosts have no blood
no flesh   no bones   no muscles   no skin as we know it
but hair which continues to grow and shed
    i do understand that most people would desire not to be forgotten
increasingly i am drawn to violence   in the early evening
          in my purple room
bad words in my books   blood in war scenes on tapestries
dead horses   impaled men and boys
people say   i am showing my ugly side
rumour is that the ghost was me because
witchcraft   soul already gone   ability to hear insects   impervious to poison
i think the exact moment of the death of love is not when its head is cut off
          and lifted to the crowd
it is a cold stone in the stomachs of the living
ghosts have no blood but the insides of their mouths are warm with breath
at dinner the candles throw unholy shadows
a cooked peacock sits on the table folded back inside its feathers
the tail fanned and rigid
      through its numerous green eyes
i watch the room zing with warm-blood people   each avoiding my face

tomorrow we will eat another beast   a spoil of our small small war
the wall against my cheek is practically ice and the night sky is loveless
what am i trying to say
fear seems heavier in winter   in my hard room
as the swans separate   and the snow comes down

beaches (11)

on night shifts
my love fantasised about
throwing himself
down the central hole of a stairwell

never underestimate
the stronghold of abstraction
fantasies can have such visual resonance

the tessellated bookshelves
orange light
what a falling angel

but that was years ago

when i wanted a house for us
a perfectly square house
i wanted to paint the house green
like a plant
with the insinuation of a flower

beaches (12)

but now
phalluses of metal and glass spike up
through a city of gentle domes

(which are very few)
often housing marble cherubs
and pious women
and glorified men
which hold no interest for me
much as i might love the domes
much as i might love the confusion
in my heart
of a concave gilded ceiling

much as we two
basically exploded each other
on winter days
very dark winter days

my choir of one
didn't we reject
the uniformity of church pews
despite really never coming near them
despite never swallowing holy air
which it transpires is edible
like a long clean stick of celery

a room can twist on its axis
or appear to

the floor gritty
and the walls wet with a moisture
that saturates bricks
i said that actually
i wanted a house on stilts
in the desert
to sleep alone on a bed of cactuses
and to stop being a liar

beaches (13)

if the city is a tight
and grubby flower
my friend is sitting
in the very centre
cutting her nails sharp
into ten translucent traps
waiting for the bee

beaches (14)

lemon juice
in your cuticle cuts
is not punishment
for anything
it is serendipity
it is one star crossing another
in a flat sky
essentially
it is god

lemon juice
lifts almost any dish
roll it on the worktop
be thankful
squeeze

speaking as a person
with almost no experience
pain can be
a gift

Acknowledgements

With thanks to *Oxford Poetry*, *Poetry London*, *Poetry Spotlight*, *Spells: 21st-Century Occult Poetry*, *The Poetry Review*, *The Rialto* and *The Scores* where these poems, or earlier versions of them, have been published.

BEACHES

First published in 2019
by Offord Road Books

www.offordroadbooks.co.uk

Typeset by Offord Road Books
Printed in the UK by Palace Printers

ISBN 978–1–999–9304–6–2

1 3 5 7 9 10 8 6 4 2

beaches

REBECCA PERRY